*With love,*
*to*
D R T H Y C
*who just finished writing a book*
*about two giants.*

The illustrations for this book were executed in ink and watercolor.
The text was set in ITC Bookman Light.
Typography by Carol Goldenberg.

Text and illustrations copyright © 1995 by Eileen Christelow.
Cover illustrations copyright © 1995 by Eileen Christelow.
All rights reserved. Published by Scholastic Inc., 557 Broadway, New York, NY 10012,
by arrangement with Clarion Books, a Houghton Mifflin Company imprint.
Printed in the U.S.A.

ISBN 0-439-78508-1

SCHOLASTIC and associated logos and designs are
trademarks and/or registered trademarks of Scholastic Inc.

10 11                    40              17 18 19 /00

WOOF?

MEOW!

# What Do Authors Do?

## BY EILEEN CHRISTELOW

SCHOLASTIC INC.
New York   Toronto   London   Auckland   Sydney
Mexico City   New Delhi   Hong Kong   Buenos Aires

Authors get ideas for books at the strangest moments!

3

When authors have ideas for books, they start to write.

Sometimes it is difficult to find the words.

Some authors write notes about what might happen in the story.
They make lists or outlines.

Some authors who write picture books are also illustrators.
Sometimes they sketch as they write. The sketches give them ideas.

Sometimes authors need more information.

So they go to libraries, historical societies, museums. . . .

They read books, old newspapers, magazines, letters, and diaries
written long ago. They take notes.

They interview people. They take more notes.

They listen and watch.

They write and write and write . . .

and cross things out . . .

throw parts of the story away . . . and start again.

Sometimes authors read their stories to their families.
Their families make suggestions.

Sometimes they read to author friends in a writers' group.
The friends make suggestions.

Sometimes authors get stuck, so they put their books away for a while.

But usually, when they are doing something else, they get unstuck.

Then they start to write again.

Authors who are also illustrators make a dummy
of the book to show how it will look with illustrations.

It can take one year, two years, or more to finish writing a manuscript!
When the stories are finished, authors send their manuscripts to publishers.

Sometimes they wait for weeks or months to hear whether the publishers
like their books.

Most authors have received rejection letters.
Some rejection letters are encouraging. Some are not.

But authors are very persistent people. They work on their manuscripts
some more. They send their manuscripts out to other publishers.

Authors are very pleased when they find a publisher!

But that is not the end of writing a book. There is still more work to do. Authors have to sign contracts (agreements) with their publishers.

Authors go to the publishers' offices to talk to their editors.

Authors work on their stories with the editors.
Editors suggest ways to make the stories better.

The authors make changes.

After the authors have made all the changes, designers decide how the book will look. They choose the size and the shape of the book. They decide which type styles to use. They design the cover.

Designers choose illustrators for the books.

Picture-book authors who do their own illustrations go over their artwork with the designer. The designer makes suggestions.

It can take four months or more to finish all of the illustrations for a picture book.

When the illustrations are finished, they need to be checked to see if anything has been left out.

When the story is set in type, it needs to be checked for mistakes.

Don't forget the dedication . . .

. . . or the author photo!

After the authors have sent all of the corrections and changes to the publisher, they won't see their books again until they are printed and bound.

When the designers have pasted up the words and the pictures on the right pages, the authors' books are sent to printers.

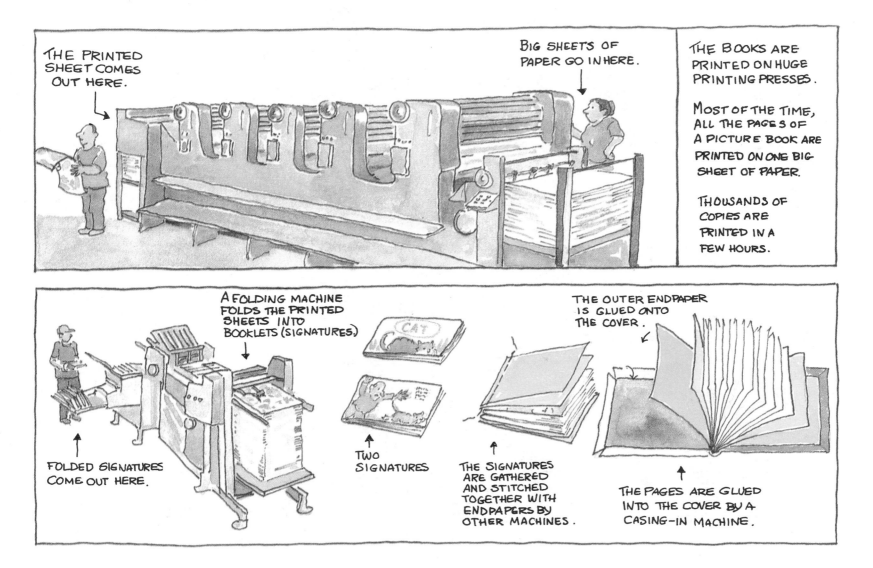

THE PRINTED SHEET COMES OUT HERE.

BIG SHEETS OF PAPER GO IN HERE.

THE BOOKS ARE PRINTED ON HUGE PRINTING PRESSES.

MOST OF THE TIME, ALL THE PAGES OF A PICTURE BOOK ARE PRINTED ON ONE BIG SHEET OF PAPER.

THOUSANDS OF COPIES ARE PRINTED IN A FEW HOURS.

A FOLDING MACHINE FOLDS THE PRINTED SHEETS INTO BOOKLETS (SIGNATURES.)

THE OUTER ENDPAPER IS GLUED ONTO THE COVER.

FOLDED SIGNATURES COME OUT HERE.

TWO SIGNATURES

THE SIGNATURES ARE GATHERED AND STITCHED TOGETHER WITH ENDPAPERS BY OTHER MACHINES.

THE PAGES ARE GLUED INTO THE COVER BY A CASING-IN MACHINE.

The printed sheets of paper go to the bindery where they are folded, gathered, trimmed, stitched, and glued into covers by huge machines.

The books are finished! Thousands of them! They are packed into boxes and sent to the publishers' warehouses.

Copies are sent to the authors.

Now that the books are published, it's a good time to celebrate!

But the authors start to worry. How are people going to find out about their books? Are people going to like them?

Magazines and newspapers review their books.
Some reviews are wonderful! Some are not.

Authors tell people about their books at schools and libraries.
They answer questions.

They autograph their books at bookstores.

But more important, authors are thinking about ideas for their next books!